SACRED DYING JOURNAL

REFLECTIONS ON EMBRACING THE END OF LIFE

MEGORY ANDERSON, PhD
and THE SACRED DYING FOUNDATION

PARACLETE PRESS
BREWSTER, MASSACHUSETTS

2017 First Printing

Sacred Dying Journal: Reflections on Embracing the End of Life

Copyright © 2017 by The Sacred Dying Foundation

ISBN 978-1-64060-007-2

The Paraclete Press name and logo (dove on cross) are trademarks of Paraclete Press, Inc.

10 9 8 7 6 5 4 3 2 1

Published by Paraclete Press
Brewster, Massachusetts
www.paracletepress.com

Printed in the United States of America

"The process of dying is a difficult one, with many fears and anxieties, but it is also a very mysterious and wondrous process. It involves both the body and the soul in the greatest transition we are ever called to make."

—Sacred Dying: Creating Rituals
for Embracing the End of Life

———————

Created by Megory Anderson, PhD,
and The Sacred Dying Foundation
San Francisco, California
www.sacreddying.org

CONTENTS

INTRODUCTION

In a class I was teaching on advanced health care directives, wills, and all the traditional paperwork one needs to capture end-of-life wishes, a woman looked down at all her notes and said, "My husband isn't going to understand what I want to have around me when I am dying; this is completely over his head. It's my women friends who will see to my spiritual needs."

And thus *Sacred Dying Journal* was born.

This journal is intended for those who wish to address their spiritual needs, even though the subject might be at times a bit uncomfortable.

This journal is a place where you can reflect on aging, illness, and preparing for the end of your life. It is a place where you can wrestle with who you are and what has meaning in your life. It's a place to capture what your wishes are for life's final journey. Writing in it can be a private experience for you—as journals often are—or it can be a time of sharing with your closest friends and loved ones. Please use it in a way that makes the most sense for you.

The journal is laid out in a way that we hope you will find helpful. There are four sections:

PART 1
Caring for the Body and the Soul
Aging, Illness, Medicine, Decline

PART 2
Sacred Dying in Time and Space
Creating the Sacred as We Die

PART 3
Legacies
Our Lives and What We Leave Behind

PART 4
Honoring the Body/Commending the Soul
When Death Happens

The questions in each section are there for your benefit, to help you think through difficult moments. You are not required to answer them at all. You may want to rephrase the questions or reflect on something else. It is totally up to you.

You may want to go through the sections in order, or you may want to skip around and do some practical writing first. Sometimes it helps to get the details going, such as the kind of music you want at your bedside, before you settle in on the more reflective questions.

There are also extra blank pages at the end of the journal. When it is time for you to go through the dying experience, those around you may wish to reflect and write about being with you during this most sacred time. It may give your loved ones an opportunity to complete the circle of life and death.

Remember, your journal will contain your wishes and desires— more so than your legal papers—because it comes from your heart.

It can help guide your loved ones in walking with you when your time comes. And it may also be a treasured part of your legacy.

Thank you for being courageous enough to explore these hard things. It will make a difference for those you love, and of course for you, in your journey.

May it be a blessing.

MEGORY ANDERSON,
Director of The Sacred Dying Foundation

SOME HELPFUL SUGGESTIONS

This journal is a combination of a workbook and a place for reflective thinking. The questions we ask are for your benefit; they serve no purpose other than to guide you in your thoughts. There are some practical questions, such as, what you would like for your funeral? And there are some philosophical questions, such as, what do you believe will happen after you die?

We suggest:

TAKE YOUR TIME. Read over the questions and let them sink in. When you feel ready to write, then begin the journal.

DON'T WORRY ABOUT TAKING THE PAGES IN ORDER. If you want to write about your legacy, then start there.

USE THE SIDEBAR SPACE to make notes or to write out your favorite poems. It's there intentionally for your "jottings."

DATE ENTRIES when you start writing and when you feel a section is complete. You may want to return to it a year from now and add some insights; date those also. You'll be grateful you did.

PART 1

Caring for the Body and the Soul
ILLNESS, AGING, MEDICINE, AND DECLINE

Are any among you suffering? They should pray. Are any cheerful? They should sing songs of praise. Are any among you sick? They should call for the elders of the church and have them pray over them, anointing them with oil in the name of the Lord. The prayer of faith will save the sick, and the Lord will raise them up; and anyone who has committed sins will be forgiven.

JAMES 5:13–15 NRSV

When it is our turn to age or to experience illness, it seems that our world becomes a medical one. Most of us will have some sort of medical condition that requires pills or procedures. We cannot stop getting older, nor can we stop our bodies from responding in certain ways. It is the cycle of life and death.

Think for a moment about how you respond when you are ill. Think also about what healing is for you. The body and the soul are entwined while we are alive, and perhaps we must learn to honor both as illness and aging come into our lives.

AGING AND ILLNESS

◎ Where are you currently on the continuum of aging or illness?

_____

_____

_____

_____

_____

_____

_____

◎ Do you feel a difference in how your body and mind work these days? How?

_____

_____

_____

_____

_____

_____

_____

14

DATED: _____

◎ Do you have an illness now that may lead to death?

_____

_____

_____

_____

_____

_____

◎ What positive things do you find in your aging or illness?

_____

_____

_____

_____

_____

_____

_____

_____

_____

I know that in life there will be sickness, devastation, disappointments, heartache–it's a given. What's not a given is the way you choose to get through it all. If you look hard enough, you can always find the bright side.

–RASHIDA JONES

DATED: _____

15

The easy path of aging is to become a thick-skinned, unbudging curmudgeon, a battle-ax. To grow soft and sweet is the harder way.

–JAMES HILLMAN

What frustrations do you feel?

DATED: _____

◎ What are you like when you are ill?

_____

_____

_____

_____

_____

_____

_____

◎ Do you like a fuss made over you? Or do you want to be left alone?

_____

_____

_____

_____

_____

_____

_____

_____

DATED: _____

When you are feeling poorly, what would you like people to know about how to be with you or help care for you?

DATED: _____

SUFFERING

Suffering is something we often think about as illness becomes more a part of our lives.

◉ How do you handle suffering?
   Do you seek pain medications at all costs?
   Are you stoic?
   Or are you somewhere in between?

Is suffering really necessary? Yes and no. If you had not suffered as you have, there would be no depth to you, no humility, no compassion.

–ECKHART TOLLE

DATED: _____

19

As cold as everything looks in winter, the sun has not forsaken us. He has only drawn away for a little, for good reasons, one of which is that we may learn that we cannot do without him.

—GEORGE MACDONALD

Where do you believe God is in the suffering?

_____

_____

_____

_____

_____

_____

_____

_____

_____

_____

_____

_____

_____

_____

_____

_____

_____

_____

_____

DATED: _____

HEALING

○ Our faith communities speak of healing. What
   does that mean to you?

O LORD my God, I called
to you for help,
and you healed me.

–PSALM 30:2 NIV

_____

_____

_____

_____

_____

_____

_____

_____

_____

_____

_____

_____

_____

_____

_____

_____

_____

_____

DATED: _____

There is comfort in knowing that you don't have to pretend anymore, that you are going to do everything within your power to heal.

—ELLEN BASS

What do you think the difference is between healing and curing?

_____

_____

_____

_____

_____

_____

_____

_____

_____

_____

_____

_____

_____

_____

_____

_____

_____

_____

_____

_____

_____

_____

DATED: _____

How do you hope your physical symptoms will change for the better?

Some days there won't be a song in your heart. Sing anyway.

—EMORY AUSTIN

DATED: _____

23

My self-healing
lies in praying for
those who have
harmed me.

—MARIANNE
WILLIAMSON

Where do you feel you most need healing?
In physical symptoms?
In spiritual symptoms?
In emotional symptoms?

_____

_____

_____

_____

_____

_____

_____

_____

_____

_____

_____

_____

_____

_____

_____

_____

_____

_____

_____

DATED: _____

TRANSITIONS

Q What does it feel like to go through transitions?

To move from here to there, sometimes there is a need to suspend the present realities; they can be a distraction.

–BIDEMI
MARK-MORDI

DATED: _____

Let go of yesterday. Let today be a new beginning and be the best that you can, and you'll get to where God wants you to be.

–JOEL OSTEEN

Is it difficult to let go of some things from the days before your decline?

_____

_____

_____

_____

_____

_____

_____

_____

_____

_____

_____

_____

_____

_____

_____

_____

_____

_____

DATED: _____

What are you looking forward to as life becomes slower?

_____

_____

_____

_____

_____

_____

_____

_____

_____

_____

_____

_____

_____

_____

_____

_____

_____

_____

The great thing about getting older is that you don't lose all the other ages you've been.

—MADELINE L'ENGLE

DATED: _____

> We do not find the meaning of life by ourselves alone—we find it with another.
>
> –THOMAS MERTON

> Every single human soul has more meaning and value than the whole of history.
>
> –NIKOLAI A. BERDYAEV

What gives you meaning today?

DATED: _____

What things do you hold on to most during times of transition? Are they for comfort? Are they for security?

I was numb, but it was from not knowing just what this new life would hold for me.

–JAMAICA KINCAID

_____

_____

_____

_____

_____

_____

_____

_____

_____

_____

_____

_____

_____

_____

_____

_____

_____

_____

DATED: _____

THINKING ABOUT DYING

Your dying may be years away or it may be upon you. Most people go through illness before they die.

◎ Do you have legal directives, with your health care advocate named and your wishes made known?

_____

_____

_____

_____

◎ Do you feel that the practical things are in place? If not, do you want to put them in place?

_____

_____

_____

_____

_____

> Death is nothing else but going home to God, the bond of love will be unbroken for all eternity.
>
> —ST. TERESA OF CALCUTTA

> Somebody should tell us, right at the start of our lives, that we are dying.
>
> —POPE PAUL VI

DATED: _____

Ⓠ Have you spoken to your family and loved ones about your wishes?

_____

_____

_____

Ⓠ How have they reacted to having "the conversation"?

_____

_____

_____

_____

_____

_____

_____

_____

_____

_____

_____

_____

_____

Tell your family what's important to you, how you want to live your life if things get hard. If they don't know what you want, how are they supposed to help you?

–CYNTHIA H.

DATED: _____

31

You matter because you are you, and you matter to the end of your life. We will do all we can not only to help you die peacefully, but also to live until you die.

—DAME CICELY SAUNDERS

What do you need in order to prepare yourself spiritually for death?

_____

_____

_____

_____

_____

_____

_____

_____

_____

_____

_____

_____

_____

_____

_____

_____

_____

_____

DATED: _____

YOUR SPIRITUAL COMPANION

A spiritual companion is someone in your life you want to walk with in this journey as you get closer to dying. He or she is your friend, companion, advocate, and voice when needed. They give you counsel, support (physical and emotional, as well as spiritual), and a commitment to be present with you as much as possible.

◉ Do you have a spiritual companion now?

_____

_____

_____

_____

◉ Have you had a spiritual companion in the past during periods of transition?

_____

_____

_____

_____

DATED: _____

33

The friend who can be silent with us in a moment of despair or confusion, who can stay with us in an hour of grief and bereavement, who can tolerate not knowing ... not healing, not curing ... that is a friend who cares.

—HENRI NOUWEN

Q How do you believe that a spiritual companion will be helpful for you?

_____

_____

_____

_____

_____

Q Can you name one person you would like to be with you?

_____

_____

Q Do they know?

_____

_____

_____

_____

34

DATED: _____

Would you want several people to be a supporting
team for you and your Spiritual Companion?

_____

_____

_____

_____

_____

When and how will you have the conversation with
them? Will you need help with that conversation?

_____

_____

_____

_____

_____

_____

_____

_____

_____

DATED: _____

35

Don't be afraid of
your fears. They're
not there to scare
you. They're there
to let you know
that something is
worth it.

—C. JOYBELL C.

If you have fears holding you back, how can your spiritual companion help you let them go?

_____

_____

_____

_____

_____

_____

_____

_____

_____

_____

_____

_____

_____

_____

_____

_____

_____

DATED: _____

How do you imagine working with a spiritual companion?
 Setting up regular meetings?
 Having informal conversations?
 Or as needed?

_____

_____

_____

_____

_____

_____

_____

_____

_____

_____

_____

_____

_____

_____

_____

DATED: _____

What we call the
beginning is often
the end.
And to make an
end is to make a
beginning.
The end is where we
start from.

—T. S. ELIOT

Can you begin to prioritize the needs you and your companion will be facing together?

_____

_____

_____

_____

_____

_____

_____

_____

_____

_____

_____

_____

_____

_____

_____

_____

DATED: _____

NOTES

DATED: _____

39

NOTES

DATED: _____

NOTES

DATED: _____

NOTES

DATED: _____

PART 2

Sacred Dying in Time and Space
CREATING THE SACRED AS WE DIE

*When it comes time to die,
be not like those whose hearts are
filled with the fear of death,
so when their time comes
they weep and pray for a little more time
to live their lives
over again in a different way.
Sing your death song,
and die like a hero going home.*

—CHIEF AUPUMUT, MOHICAN

When dying begins to happen, it is time to turn all attention to the person in the bed. This is the experience that will come to each of us, and we hope that it comes in a peaceful, sacred way. And despite all the activity happening among doctors, nurses, caregivers, and loved ones, the experience of dying belongs to the dying person.

Help your loved ones know what you will want. Think now about what is important to you, so that when it comes time for you to go through your dying experience they can help you. Those who care for you will listen to you and try to honor your wishes.

Your sacred space is
where you can find
yourself again and
again.

-JOSEPH CAMPBELL

YOUR SACRED SPACE

When dying starts to happen, the space around you is very important. Clutter can be cleared. Special things that have meaning for you can be brought in. Sounds, smells, images, and touch are all-important now. Think about what these things might be for you.

What items of special meaning do you want in your room?

_____

_____

_____

_____

_____

_____

_____

_____

_____

_____

DATED: _____

What items do you want near your bed to look at or to hold? Flowers? Candles? Photographs?

Sacred spaces can be created in any environment.

—CHRISTY TURLINGTON

_____

_____

_____

_____

_____

_____

_____

_____

_____

_____

_____

_____

_____

_____

_____

_____

_____

_____

DATED: _____

45

Tread softly as you draw near to the bedside of a dying one, for the space around her is holy ground. Speak in hushed tones, with awe and reverence, as you would in a cathedral.

–JENNIFER WORTH

A QUIET SPACE

What kind of environment is important to you? Peaceful? Quiet? Social?

_____

_____

_____

_____

_____

What can you tell your spiritual companion about the people you want—or don't want—around you?

_____

_____

_____

_____

_____

_____

DATED: _____

BOOKS

◎ Do you like people to read to you?

_____

_____

_____

_____

_____

_____

◎ What are your favorite books?

_____

_____

_____

_____

_____

_____

_____

DATED: _____

I cannot sleep
unless
I am surrounded
by books.

–JORGE LUIS
BORGES

47

Music can minister to minds diseased, pluck from the memory a rooted sorrow, raze out the written troubles of the brain, and with its sweet oblivious antidote, cleanse the full bosom of all perilous stuff that weighs upon the heart.

—WILLIAM SHAKESPEARE

MUSIC

◎ Is it important for you to have music?

_____

_____

_____

_____

_____

_____

_____

◎ What kind of music do you like most?

_____

_____

_____

_____

_____

_____

_____

DATED: _____

List some of your favorite music/songs.

DATED: _____

COMFORT

Dying often takes days or weeks. How do you like to be comforted and reassured?

_____

_____

_____

_____

_____

_____

_____

_____

_____

_____

_____

_____

_____

_____

Whether you've seen angels floating around your bedroom or just found a ray of hope at a lonely moment, choosing to believe that something unseen is caring for you can be a life-shifting exercise.

—MARTHA BECK

50

DATED: _____

VISIONS

The dying often have visions of loved ones waiting for them, or sometimes of holy people offering assistance.

⊙ Do you want or expect to have visions of loved ones as you prepare to die? If so, who might you see?

_____

_____

_____

_____

_____

_____

_____

_____

_____

_____

_____

_____

_____

_____

The mother of the dying child looked down at the bed and said softly,

"Darling, perhaps Jesus will be coming soon to take you to heaven."

"Oh Mummy. He's been here for days. We're having a wonderful time."

—MEGORY ANDERSON

DATED: _____

No one can say that
death found in me a
willing comrade, or
that I went easily.

—CASSANDRA
CLARE

You Can Say No

◉ Is there something you don't want to happen as you
die?

_____

_____

_____

_____

_____

_____

_____

_____

_____

_____

_____

_____

_____

_____

_____

_____

_____

_____

_____

DATED: _____

If there were a perfect place you would want to die, where would you want it to be?

 At home?
 In a place where you are taken care of?
 A favorite city?
 In nature?

When it's my time, take me out into the garden. I want to smell the flowers and be surrounded by the earth.

−TOM B.

DATED: _____

Abraham
breathed his last
and died in a
good old age, an
old man and full
of years, and was
gathered to his
people.

—GENESIS 25:8
NRSV

If there were a perfect way for you to die, what would it be?

_____

_____

_____

_____

_____

_____

_____

_____

_____

_____

_____

_____

_____

_____

_____

_____

_____

DATED: _____

NOTES

DATED: _____

NOTES

DATED: _____

NOTES

DATED: _____

NOTES

DATED: _____

PART 3

Legacies

Our Lives and What
We Leave Behind

*Everyone must leave something behind when he dies. . . .
Something your hand touched some way so your soul has
somewhere to go when you die. . . . It doesn't matter what
you do, so long as you change something from the way
it was before you touched it into something that's like you
after you take your hands away.*

—RAY BRADBURY

When people think of legacies, they think of possessions or trusts for future generations. These are things that go into your will. The legacy I am speaking of, on the other hand, is a reflection on your life and how you have made a difference in the hearts and memories of those whom you have touched. Because you have touched lives. You have made a difference.

> You were created,
> fashioned and
> designed in a special
> form to leave in the
> world something that
> did not exist before
> you were born!
>
> –ISRAELMORE AYIVOR

LOOKING BACK

Some people have written biographies of themselves.

◎ Have you anything already written? Are some of the things still around and available? Poems? Letters? A diary?

DATED: _____

Thinking Back

◎ What are some of the accomplishments you value the most?

_____

_____

_____

_____

_____

_____

_____

_____

_____

_____

_____

_____

_____

_____

_____

_____

_____

_____

_____

_____

Legacy is more than leaving possessions behind. It's about investing in people with passion and integrity through leadership and love.

—FARSHAD ASL

DATED: _____

61

The days, months and years eventually reveal, like a Polaroid, a clear picture of how significant events and decisions eventually shape our lives.

–HODA KOTB

Q What have been the most significant events in your life?

_____

_____

_____

_____

_____

_____

_____

_____

_____

_____

_____

_____

_____

_____

_____

_____

DATED: _____

STRUGGLES AND JOYS

What have been your deepest struggles?

_____

_____

_____

_____

_____

_____

_____

_____

_____

_____

_____

_____

_____

_____

_____

_____

_____

_____

_____

DATED: _____

Joy is prayer–Joy
is strength–Joy is
love–Joy is a net of
love by which you
can catch souls. She
gives most who
gives with Joy.

–ST. TERESA OF
CALCUTTA

Q What have been your most cherished joys?

DATED: _____

LOVE

◉ Who have you loved?

_____

_____

_____

_____

_____

_____

◉ Who has loved you?

_____

_____

_____

_____

_____

_____

_____

The most important thing in life is to learn how to give out love, and let it come in.

—MORRIE SCHWARTZ

DATED: _____

65

YOUR GIFTS

What are the gifts you have been given?

_____

_____

_____

_____

_____

_____

_____

_____

_____

_____

_____

_____

_____

_____

_____

When I stand before God at the end of my life, I would hope that I would not have a single bit of talent left, and could say, 'I used everything you gave me'.

—ERMA BOMBECK

DATED: _____

How have you used them?

Everyone has unique
gifts and talents.
What you love is
what you're gifted at.

−BARBARA SHER

DATED: _____

> Carve your name on hearts, not tombstones. A legacy is etched into the minds of others and the stories they share about you.
>
> –SHANNON L. ALDER

OTHERS

How do you hope people will remember you?

_____

_____

_____

_____

_____

_____

_____

_____

_____

_____

_____

_____

_____

_____

_____

DATED: _____

What do you hope they will have forgotten or forgiven?

Everyone has need
to be forgiven.

−GEORGE HERBERT

DATED: _____

> The best part of
> the journey is the
> surprise and wonder
> along the way.
>
> –KEN POIROT

SURPRISES

◉ What are the surprises that changed your life?
Uncertainties? Disappointments? Successes?
Delights?

_____

_____

_____

_____

_____

_____

_____

_____

_____

_____

_____

_____

_____

_____

DATED: _____

LOOKING FORWARD

Q What do you hope you will leave the world?
In your accomplishments?
In your relationships?
In how you lived your life?

I slept and I dreamed
that life is all joy. I woke
and I saw that life is all
service. I served and I
saw that service is joy.

–KAHLIL GIBRAN

_____

_____

_____

_____

_____

_____

_____

_____

_____

_____

_____

_____

_____

DATED: _____

Spiritual Insights

Q What spiritual insights have you, finally, had?

We must show our Christian colours if we are to be true to Jesus Christ.

–C. S. LEWIS

Take a moment to think of everything you're proud of about yourself and your life. Then ask yourself if you would have any of this without God's permission and aid? Give credit where credit is due; praise and thank Him, not yourself.

–ST. FRANCIS OF ASSISI

DATED: _____

Who do you think has learned from you?

_____

_____

_____

_____

_____

_____

_____

_____

_____

_____

_____

_____

_____

_____

_____

_____

_____

_____

_____

As you become more present in your own life, you will begin to enlighten others by your example.

−GERMANY KENT

DATED: _____

73

I plan to live my own
way. Hopefully, it is
as per God's way.

−FAKEER ISHAVARDAS

Q What are the spiritual understandings you feel you
have lived your life by?

_____

_____

_____

_____

_____

_____

_____

_____

_____

_____

_____

_____

_____

_____

_____

_____

_____

_____

_____

DATED: _____

TOUCHSTONES

◉ What specific items or touchstones do you want to pass on to someone special. A letter? A small item? A religious item?

_____

_____

_____

_____

_____

_____

_____

◉ Who are the recipients?

_____

_____

_____

_____

_____

_____

DATED: _____

One must know not just how to accept a gift, but with what grace to share it.

—MAYA ANGELOU

75

NOTES

_____

_____

_____

_____

_____

_____

_____

_____

_____

_____

_____

_____

_____

_____

_____

_____

DATED: _____

NOTES

NOTES

DATED: _____

PART 4

Honoring the Body/Commending the Soul
WHEN DEATH HAPPENS

Nicodemus, who had at first come to Jesus by night, also came, bringing a mixture of myrrh and aloes, weighing about a hundred pounds. They took the body of Jesus and wrapped it with the spices in linen cloths, according to the burial custom of the Jews. Now there was a garden in the place where he was crucified, and in the garden there was a new tomb in which no one had ever been laid. And so, because it was the Jewish day of Preparation, and the tomb was nearby, they laid Jesus there.
JOHN 19:39–42 NRSV

Most faith traditions know what to do when death happens. There are customs to honor the body, which include washing and purifying it, getting it ready for others to say their goodbyes, and preparing it for burial or cremation.

The ritual of preparing the body, and those to whom the job falls, are considered very honorable.

Faith traditions also know that sometimes it takes prayers to commend the soul on its final journey. As it separates from the body, many believe that the soul needs encouragement to find its way home.

Funerals are also important, not only for loved ones, but also for the person who has died. These rituals honor the end of a unique life, provide the means for laying the body to rest while offering prayers for the soul.

When we face
death, really face
it, we realize that
only love matters.

–MARTY RUBIN

REFLECTIONS ON LIFE'S END

What are your thoughts about your life on earth as it comes to an end?

_____

_____

_____

_____

_____

_____

_____

_____

_____

_____

_____

_____

_____

_____

DATED: _____

How do you want God to be present with you as you go through your death?

_____

_____

_____

_____

_____

_____

_____

_____

_____

_____

_____

_____

_____

_____

_____

_____

_____

_____

Whether it's a Christian or a non-Christian, there's nothing like suffering to show us how small, needy, and not in control we are. Suffering has a way of sobering us up to the realization that we can't make it on our own, that we need help, that we're broken.

—TULLIAN TCHIVIDJIAN

DATED: _____

81

When you learn
your lessons, the
pain goes away.

—ELISABETH
KÜBLER-ROSS

Do you think suffering must be a part of death?

_____

_____

_____

_____

_____

Why?

_____

_____

_____

_____

_____

_____

_____

_____

DATED: _____

⦿ What do you believe happens when your body dies?

_____

_____

_____

_____

_____

_____

_____

_____

_____

_____

_____

_____

_____

_____

_____

_____

_____

_____

The time of my departure has come. I have fought the good fight, I have finished the race, I have kept the faith.

—2 TIMOTHY 4:6-7

DATED: _____

Seeing death as the end of life is like seeing the horizon as the end of the ocean.

—DAVID SEARLS

How do you feel attached to your body now as it declines?

_____

_____

_____

_____

_____

_____

_____

Are you ready to let go of your body?

_____

_____

_____

_____

_____

DATED: _____

What are your beliefs about the afterlife?

_____

_____

_____

_____

_____

_____

_____

_____

_____

_____

_____

_____

_____

_____

_____

_____

_____

There is a place called "heaven" where the good here unfinished is completed; and where the stories unwritten, and the hopes unfulfilled, are continued.

–J.R.R. TOLKIEN

DATED: _____

85

You don't believe in
the soul until you
feel it straining to
escape the body.

−GLEN DUNCAN

What do you think will happen to your self/your soul in the afterlife?

DATED: _____

Do you think that the soul finds its home right away? Why or why not?

In culture after culture, people believe that the soul lives on after death, that rituals can change the physical world and divine the truth.

–STEPHEN PINKER

DATED: _____

Please, please
tell me I'll see my
husband in heaven.
Why would God give
us this love and not
have it be forever?

–DORIS K.

Q Will you hope to be reunited with loved ones? If so, which ones and why?

DATED: _____

NOTES

DATED: _____

Notes

DATED: _____

PRACTICAL THINGS

ONCE DEATH HAPPENS

Watching a peaceful death of a human being reminds us of a falling star; one of a million lights in a vast sky that flares up for a brief moment only to disappear into the endless night forever.

–ELISABETH
KÜBLER-ROSS

Do you want people called to come to your bedside during this time of transition? If so, who are they?

_____

_____

_____

_____

_____

_____

Do you have special prayers/readings you want said?

_____

_____

_____

_____

DATED: _____

Is there a favorite song or hymn you want sung?

_____

_____

_____

_____

_____

_____

_____

Are there times when you have been present for a loved one or a patient at the moment of death?

_____

_____

_____

_____

_____

_____

_____

Goin' home, goin' home, I'm just going home. Quiet-like, slip away—I'll be going home.

–WILLIAM ARMS FISHER

DATED: _____

93

Some people have described loving light filling the room or a sudden change in room temperature. Or there may be a heaviness in the air which takes time to clear, or there may be other strange phenomena such as clocks stopping at the moment of death, pets behaving out of character, or birds and butterflies appearing at the window.

—DYING MATTERS
COALITION

How was it for you during this very liminal time?

_____

_____

_____

_____

_____

_____

_____

_____

_____

_____

_____

_____

_____

_____

_____

_____

DATED: _____

Did you sense any changes—subtle or otherwise—
as the soul left the body?

_____

_____

_____

_____

_____

_____

_____

_____

_____

_____

_____

_____

_____

_____

_____

_____

DATED: _____

WASHING THE BODY

May this water
cleanse you and wash
you clean of pain and
sorrow and suffering.

—TRADITIONAL
BLESSING

It is the tradition in most cultures and faith traditions for the body to remain in the deathbed room for some time, and to be washed, purified, and clothed.

Ⓠ Who would you like to wash and purify your body? Loved ones? Family? Friends? A caregiver? A nurse? Someone neutral?

_____

_____

_____

_____

_____

Ⓠ Is there a special prayer or song you would like used while they wash you?

_____

_____

_____

_____

DATED: _____

CLOTHING

What clothing do you wish to be dressed in after your body has been washed?

_____

_____

_____

_____

_____

_____

Is there something you would like to hold in your hands? A prayer book? Beads?

_____

_____

_____

_____

_____

_____

The two of us dressed her in a beautiful blue caftan and placed white calla lilies in her arms. All the pain and suffering had left her face and finally, after all these months, she was at peace.

–ELIZABETH R.

DATED: _____

Jewelry? My favorite hat? No thank you. Put pictures of each of my children around me in the coffin. I want them to be with me as I go to God.

–CAROL S.

Do you have something you would like to place beside you on the bed? Pictures? Flowers?

_____

_____

_____

_____

_____

_____

_____

Do you want to be buried or cremated this way?

_____

_____

_____

_____

_____

_____

_____

DATED: _____

Do you have other specific instructions on how you wish to be laid out?

_____

_____

_____

_____

_____

_____

_____

_____

_____

_____

_____

_____

_____

_____

_____

_____

_____

The two of us dressed her in a beautiful blue caftan and placed white calla lilies in her arms. All the pain and suffering had left her face and finally, after all these months, she was at peace.

–ELIZABETH R.

DATED: _____

THE FUNERAL

Some say that the funeral or memorial service is for those who are left behind. Some say that the continuum of care is not complete until your body is laid to rest. What are your thoughts on this?

_____

_____

_____

_____

_____

_____

_____

_____

_____

_____

_____

_____

_____

The biggest problem is the funerals that don't exist. People call the funeral home, they pick up the body, they mail the ashes to you, no grief, no happiness, no remembrance, no nothing.

—CAITLIN DOUGHTY

DATED: _____

Funeral Home

○ Do you have a funeral home selected to take care of your body?

_____

_____

_____

○ Do the funeral directors have instructions as to what you want?

_____

_____

_____

○ Do you have a coffin chosen if you are to be buried? Who has the instructions?

_____

_____

_____

DATED: _____

We kept my husband at home after he died. People came to pay their respects, sat silently with his body right there in the bedroom, and we talked about how they used to do this in the olden days. It gave me great comfort.

–DIANE B.

Ⓠ Do you have an urn chosen if you are to be cremated? Who has the instructions?

_____

_____

_____

_____

_____

_____

_____

Ⓠ Do you want a home funeral, where your body stays at home until the burial, rather than being taken to a funeral home?

_____

_____

_____

_____

_____

DATED: _____

VIEWING

◎ Is it your wish to have a viewing before the funeral?
Where?

_____

_____

_____

_____

_____

◎ Will you want a formal liturgy for the viewing?

_____

_____

_____

_____

_____

_____

_____

DATED: _____

◎ What are the specific prayers and rituals you want to use?

_____

_____

_____

_____

_____

_____

_____

_____

_____

_____

_____

◎ Is that information available? Who has it?

_____

_____

_____

DATED: _____

ULTIMATE RESTING PLACE

◉ Do you have a loved one who has died where you remember visiting the graveside or visit it now?

_____

_____

_____

_____

_____

_____

_____

_____

◉ Is having a place people can visit important to you?

_____

_____

_____

_____

_____

DATED: _____

My mother died when I was ten, and every Sunday my father and I went to the cemetery to take her flowers. My father would talk to her as he fussed over the grave. It helped to know she would always be there, waiting.

–DAVID R.

105

The notion of burial had always struck him as stifling and cold. He liked the Indian way better, setting the bodies up high, as if passing them to the heavens.

—MICHAEL PUNKE

What are your preferences for where your body is to be laid to rest?

_____

_____

_____

_____

_____

_____

_____

Do you want to be in a place where others can visit, remember, and honor you, such as a cemetery?

_____

_____

_____

_____

_____

_____

106

DATED: _____

◉ Do you want to be in a place where loved ones are buried?

_____

_____

_____

_____

_____

_____

_____

◉ Who has your instructions?

_____

_____

_____

_____

_____

_____

_____

_____

_____

DATED: _____

BURIAL

For as much as I hate the cemetery, I've been grateful it's here, too. I miss my wife. It's easier to miss her at a cemetery, where she's never been anything but dead, than to miss her in all the places where she was alive.

—JOHN SCALZI

Q Where is your plot?

_____

_____

_____

_____

_____

_____

_____

Q Is there a family plot? A military plot?

_____

_____

_____

_____

_____

_____

_____

DATED: _____

Do you want a "green/natural burial"?

_____

_____

_____

_____

_____

_____

_____

_____

_____

_____

_____

_____

_____

_____

_____

_____

_____

_____

_____

You must teach your children that the ground beneath their feet is the ashes of your grandfathers. So that they will respect the land, tell your children that the earth is rich with the lives of our kin.

—CHIEF SEATTLE

DATED: _____

It is the will of God
and Nature that these
mortal bodies be laid
aside…

–BENJAMIN FRANKLIN

CREMATION

◉ Who is to receive your ashes?

_____

_____

_____

_____

_____

◉ Do you have a specific location where you'd like
your ashes to be placed or scattered?

_____

_____

_____

_____

_____

_____

_____

DATED: _____

◉ If not, who do you want to decide this?

_____

_____

_____

_____

_____

_____

_____

◉ Who has your instructions?

_____

_____

_____

_____

_____

_____

_____

_____

DATED: _____

111

I'm donating my organs to science. Will they want an old lady's kidney? I have no idea, but it's my way of giving something back.

–PATRICIA B.

ALTERNATIVES TO TRADITIONAL BURIALS

◉ There are several alternatives to traditional burials, including:

Green or eco-friendly burials
Burial at sea/coral reefs
Freezing
Changing the body into gems or other substances
Organ/research donation

DATED: _____

Would an alternative such as one of these be something you would like?

DATED: _____

Sleep on now, and
take your rest.

—MATTHEW 26:45

THE FUNERAL SERVICE

◉ Do you want a funeral service—with your body present, either in a coffin or an urn?

_____

_____

_____

◉ Would you rather have a memorial service—with your body not present?

_____

_____

_____

◉ Would you prefer that nothing be done at all?

_____

_____

_____

DATED: _____

Tell us about the funeral or memorial service itself.

Lord, now lettest thou thy servant depart in peace, according to thy word.

–LUKE 2:29 KJV

DATED: _____

115

I wonder how you say
goodbye to someone
forever?

—ANN M. MARTIN

◉ Who do you wish to be in charge of planning the service?

_____

_____

_____

_____

_____

_____

◉ Have you done any planning so far? If yes, where are these instructions or plans?

_____

_____

_____

_____

_____

_____

DATED: _____

These are some things that traditionally make up a funeral or memorial service. If you would like, you can write out your preferences here.

Location of service:

_____

Officiant(s):

1. _____

2. _____

Other service participants:

1. _____

2. _____

3. _____

Readings:

1. _____

2. _____

3. _____

Readers:

1. _____

2. _____

3. _____

DATED: _____

Sermon/Homily: _____

_____

Eulogy/Words of Remembrance:

1. _____

2. _____

3. _____

Hymns or songs you would like included:

_____

_____

_____

_____

_____

_____

Musicians:

1. _____

2. _____

3. _____

DATED: _____

Other preferences:

1. _____

2. _____

3. _____

_____

_____

_____

_____

_____

_____

◉ Is there to be a reception afterward? Where?

_____

_____

_____

_____

_____

_____

DATED: _____

Death is in the
good-bye.

−ANNE SEXTON

JOURNEY TO THE CEMETERY OR SCATTERING PLACE

Do you wish everyone to travel to the cemetery if you are to be buried?

_____

_____

_____

_____

_____

Blessed are they
that mourn: for they
shall be comforted.

−MATTHEW 5:4 KJV

If not, who do you wish to be present?

_____

_____

_____

_____

_____

DATED: _____

⊙ If there is a scattering of ashes, have you a
designated place? Where?

_____

_____

_____

_____

⊙ Are there any readings or prayers you wish to be
said?

_____

_____

_____

_____

_____

_____

_____

_____

_____

_____

DATED: _____

FINAL THOUGHTS

Though lovers be
lost, love shall not;
And death shall have
no dominion.

–DYLAN THOMAS

We were promised
sufferings. They were
part of the program.
We were even told,
"Blessed are they
that mourn," and
I accept it. I've got
nothing that I hadn't
bargained for.

–C. S. LEWIS

◎ What are your thoughts about leaving your loved ones?

DATED: _____

After all these thoughts, wishes, and reflections, is there anything else that you think is important?

_____

_____

_____

_____

_____

_____

_____

_____

_____

_____

_____

_____

_____

_____

_____

_____

_____

_____

_____

_____

I was learning that when you're with someone who is dying, you may need to celebrate the past, live the present, and mourn the future all at the same time."

—WILL SCHWALBE

To every thing there is a season, and a time to every purpose under the heaven:
A time to be born, and a time to die.

—ECCLESIASTES 3:1–2 KJV

DATED: _____

REFLECTIONS

For Those Who Keep Watch with You

DATED: _____